G000135701

In Praise of Ginger

A recipe book

Alison Murray

First published 2007
This revised edition 2009

Published by All2knit
High Rising,
Northdown Road,
Bideford, Devon,
EX39 3LP
(www.all2knit.co.uk)

All rights reserved. No part of this publication may be
reproduced, stored in a retrieval system or transmitted, in
any form or by any means, electronic, mechanical,
photocopying, recording, or otherwise, without the prior
written permission of the publishers.

ISBN 978-0-9561715-0-4

Artwork & Print by B.A.P.S. Publishing Ltd, 01237 425178

In Praise of Ginger . . . mostly

Ginger is the root of all things good,
Like gingercake and ginger pud;
There's savoury ginger and ginger sweet,
Oh nothing compares to its sensual heat.
There's crystalline ginger, naughty but nice,
Or rhubarb and ginger, or ginger ice;
There's ginger slices and ginger sauce,
And good old ginger beer of course.
Then there's ginger biscuits and ginger bread,
But there's one kind of ginger that everyone dreads;
It's obvious really, if you stop and think . . .
It's that ginger nut on The Weakest Link!

Mike Jubb

Contents

(All recipes included in this book have been included as given but we can accept no responsibility for any errors therein)

Introduction

Back in 2005 we decided to organise a local community-knitting project to make the worlds largest knitted Christmas tree. The aim was to encourage people to take up the craft of knitting and show that knitting can be fun. We wanted to encourage every one of all ages to take part

We started to publicise it in The Western Morning News which resulted in numerous phone calls from across the whole of the West Country from Bristol to Lands End. Soon we were sending out details to hundreds of knitters.

Many Saturdays were spent knitting and talking to people at Atlantic Village Shopping outlet in Devon, which was to be the venue for the tree. The idea was to promote interest in the project. This resulted in many holidaymakers becoming interested and soon we had knitters from across the whole of the UK becoming involved.

Magazine interest, word of mouth and the Internet added knitters from across the world. Numbers quickly grew to over 700 knitters with ages ranging from 4 to 102 years of age.

We visited our local schools, sheltered housing groups and got people knitting on the beach in the summer. Such was the interest that a number of new knitting groups were formed.

The tree was successfully displayed as planned at Atlantic Village in November and December 2005 where it raised over £13,000 for The North Devon Hospice.

The following winter it was also displayed at Birmingham NEC, Minehead Festival of Trees and The Eden Project in Cornwall.

Having created such interest with this first project we found that as soon as it came to an end there were requests for what to do next and this is how the Gingerbread House idea originated. It was to be a life size house, exterior and interior, in its own garden, a much bigger and more challenging project than the tree.

We wanted the knitters to think of, and create, 3-dimensional knitting and give everyone free range with colour and texture. Cakes of all sizes, sweets, 3D furniture, utensils, flowers, gingerbread men are examples of what was needed. We also needed coloured squares, the building blocks of the house.

The response was overwhelming with finished knitting arriving from all over the UK and abroad. We received Plymouth rock from Devon and gingerbread men from Portugal

The finished project was displayed at Atlantic Village throughout the summer of 2007. It created quite a stir with nationwide interest. Thousands of people came to see it and it was also featured on The Graham Norton Show as well as being used as a fashion shoot by The White Stuff fashion company.

Shortly after the house came out of Atlantic Village it began a national tour of the UK as a feature of the ICHF exhibitions. Between September 2007 and April 2008 it visited Exeter, Harrogate, Brighton, Cardiff, Glasgow,

Birmingham and Liverpool. At every venue it got an amazing reception and was regularly featured on the local television and in the local papers.

In 2008 it appeared in the America Craft magazine which led to it being featured on The Martha Stewart television show in America.

As at the date of this edition the house is about to leave for an exhibition in Paris in February 2009. It is then due to visit Newcastle at the start of April and in the summer of 2009 it will be at Coldharbour Working Mill, Uffculme in Devon.

Whenever the Tree or the House were displayed they raised money for charity. To date they raised £20,000 for the North Devon Hospice and £16,000 for Great Ormond Street Hospital for Sick Children. The public has been very generous in helping us to raise so much.

Both projects have given enormous enjoyment to all the knitters and helpers who have contributed and it is a credit to all their hard work that is has given such pleasure to the many thousand of people who have already seen the projects across the UK and will continue to do so at future exhibitions.

Our knitters have also contributed to this cookery book. We asked knitters to send us their favourite recipes, which included ginger. This book is only able to contain a selection of the many, many recipes we received but we would like to thank every one of you for your recipes, we hope there is something for everyone.

Thanks again to the fantastic knitters, helpers and contributors without whom we could never have created the amazing "Largest Knitted Christmas Tree" and "Giant Knitted Gingerbread House".

Alison and Ann Murray
February 2009

4

Gingerbread and Cakes

Doreens favourite Gingerbread

Ingredients

3 Cups Self Raising Flour
3 Teaspoonfuls Ground Ginger
2 Teaspoonfuls Bicarbonate of Soda
1 1/2 Cups Golden Caster Sugar

1/2lb Margarine
4 Tablespoonfuls of Syrup
2 Cups Boiling Milk

Method

Put all ingredients in a bowl and mix lightly. Pour over boiling water and mix until smooth. Pour into a greased and lined 12" by 9" tin.
Bake for 3/4 hour (or until spongy when touched in the middle) Leave in the tin over-night before cutting.

Doreen Jennings, Sandy, Beds

Fruit Gingerbread

Ingredients

125g / 4oz Butter
75g / 3oz Brown Sugar
10ml / 2tsp Ground Ginger
2 1/2ml / 1/2tsp Ground Nutmeg
25g / 1oz Flaked Almonds
5ml / 1tsp Bicarbonate of Soda

125g / 4oz Dark Treacle
225g / 8oz Flour
50g / 2oz Rolled Oats
75g / 3oz Sultanas
175ml / 6 fl oz Sour Cream
3 Eggs

Method

Put butter sugar, treacle in saucepan, heat till butter melts, set aside to cool slightly then beat in eggs one at a time. Sift flour, soda, spices into a bowl then stir in oats, sultanas and almonds. Add butter mixture and sour cream, stir well. Line 18cm/7" square baking tin with double thickness greased greaseproof paper.
Spoon in batter, cook 50 min to 1 hour at 180°C/350°F Gas Mark 4.
Cook until a knife inserted comes out clean. Cool, on wire rack.

Helena Turner, Launceston

Lemon Gingerbread

Ingredients

3oz Marge
3 Tablespoons Golden Syrup   3oz Golden Granulated Sugar
1^{1}/2 Level Teaspoon Ground Ginger   6oz Self Raising Flour
1 Level Teaspoon Mixed Spice   1 Egg
4 Fluid Oz Water   1 Level Tsp Bicarbonate of Soda
1 Tbsp freshly squeezed lemon juice and grated rind.

Method

Place marge, sugar and syrup into a pan and warm gently till dissolved.
Sieve all other ingredients into a bowl and stir in syrup mixture.
Add the beaten eggs and stir until smooth. Pour into greased and lined 7"
cake tin. Bake 45 - 55 minutes at 350°F / 180°C and cool in tin.

Jennifer Blowfield, Oadby, Lancs

Scotch Gingerbread

*For an old fashioned, sticky, black gingerbread, that keeps well and is
best eaten a few days after cooking*

Ingredients

1/2lb Butter or Margarine   1/2lb Soft Brown Sugar
1/2 to 3/4lb Black Treacle   2 Eggs - beaten
2 Tbsp Ground Ginger   1/2lb Flour
1 Tbsp Powdered Cinnamon   1 Tsp Bicarbonate of Soda
1/2 Tsp of Hot Milk

Method

Cream the butter with the sugar, add the treacle, eggs and dry ingredients
but not the bicarbonate of soda. Dissolve this in the warm milk and add it
last. Bake in a well greased round 18cm / 7^{1}/2" tin for 2 - 2^{1}/2 hours in a
slow oven (300°F / 150°C Gas Mark 2). Leave in tin until cold. Cut like
an ordinary cake. Wrap in foil.

Rosemary Hobson, Wells, Somerset

Quick Gingerbread

Ingredients

6oz Flour   2oz Margarine or Lard
2oz Bicarbonate of Soda   2oz Golden Syrup
5fl oz Milk   1 Tsp Baking Soda
1 Tsp Powdered Ginger   Pinch of Salt

Method

Grease an ovenproof tin, mix flour, sugar, ginger and salt. Warm fat and
syrup with soda in a pan, add milk and other dry ingredients.
Bake in a moderate oven for approximately half an hour.

Mrs Ivy Voysey

Sticky Top Gingerbread

Ingredients

8oz plain flour   4oz margarine
1 egg   4oz brown sugar
3 - 4 level tsp ground ginger   1 level tsp bicarbonate of soda
8oz syrup and black treacle, mixed

Method

Grease and line a 7" square tin with greaseproof paper. Sieve the flour,
ginger and bicarbonate together. Melt marge, sugar and syrup in a pan on
low heat stirring all the time. Add milk when cooled a little. Beat egg and
add to liquid mixture when cool then stir in dry ingredients. Pour into tin.
Cook in a slow oven (Gas mark 2) for about an hour until springy and
leaving sides of tin. Keep in a cake tin for a day to become sticky.

Mrs Phyllis Bamforth

Almond Gingerbread

Ingredients

7oz self raising flour
1/2 tsp ground ginger
1/2 tsp mixed spice
4oz soft brown sugar
1oz minced crystallised ginger
1oz chopped glace cherries

1oz ground almonds
5oz butter
5oz treacle
Grated rind of 1/2 a lemon
2 large or 3 small eggs

Method

Pre-heat oven to 350°F (gas mark 3 - 4). Sift the flour with the almonds, ginger and spice into a basin. Place the butter, treacle and syrup in a saucepan and heat gently until butter has melted. Add to the dry ingredients and beat well.
Stir in the ginger, cherries, lemon rind and eggs, beaten well. Pour into a round 7" cake tin smoothly lined with greased paper. Bake on middle shelf of oven for about 1 1/4 hours.
Leave in tin for about 30 min before turning out onto a wire rack to cool. When quite cool wrap in foil or greaseproof paper and store in an airtight tin several days before cutting.

NOTE. To make this cake successfully be careful not to open the oven door until cake is nearly ready or it may fall in the centre. I would make it the weekend before it is required.

Mrs J Davie, Salcombe

Apple Gingerbread

Ingredients

4oz (100g) golden syrup
2oz (50g) Demerara sugar
3oz (75g) butter
6oz (150g) self raising flour
1 level tbsp granulated sugar

2 level tsp ginger
$1/4$ level tsp cinnamon
1 large egg
8oz (200g) cooking apples
2 tbsp water

7" x 11" shallow tin, greased and base lined.

Method

Melt together syrup, Demerara sugar and butter.
Sieve together flour, ginger and cinnamon.
Peel and core apples. Cook until soft with water and ginger. Cool.
Mix all together with a large egg.
Cook at 180°C, gas mark 4, for 40 minutes until golden brown. Cool on a
wire rack.

Gill Gordon, Petrockstowe

Norfolk Gingerbread

Ingredients

6oz self raising flour
2 tsp ground ginger
$2^1/2$oz granulated sugar
$1/2$tsp bicarbonate of soda

3oz butter
2 tbsp golden syrup
1 egg
2 tbsp milk

Method

Sieve the flour and ginger together, then rub in the butter.
Stir in sugar. Beat syrup and egg together. Warm milk and stir in the
bicarbonate of soda then add to the egg mixture. Beat well and pour into
the dry ingredients. Mix well. Put into a 6" cake tin, greased beforehand.
Cook at 350°F for approx 1 hour 10 minutes. Turn out onto a tray to cool.

Mrs. P. Cattle, Rickmansworth

Orange Gingerbread

Ingredients

12oz plain flour
4oz butter or margarine
3oz chopped candied orange peel
1/2 orange
1/2 tsp cinnamon
Pinch of salt and cayenne pepper

4oz light brown sugar
4oz golden syrup
2 eggs
1/2 tsp ground ginger
1/2 tsp bicarbonate of soda

Method

Sieve together the flour, spices, salt and pepper. Rub in butter until mixture is fine like breadcrumbs. Stir in sugar. Heat syrup until it is thin and runny then stir into the mixture. Whisk eggs lightly and beat into cakes mixture. Grate the rind and squeeze juice from the orange, add to the mixture along with the candied peel. Pour into a 7" tin and bake for 1 hour at 325°F. Turn out onto a wire tray to cool before eating

Mrs. P. Cattle, Rickmansworth

Ginger Drop Cake

Ingredients

8 oz Flour
2 oz Sugar
1 Tsp Ground Ginger
1/2 Tsp Bicarbonate of Soda
3 Tbsp (6 oz) Lyles Golden Syrup

2 oz Butter
1 Egg
1/2 Tsp Mixed spice
2 Tbsp Milk

Method

Melt sugar and butter on stove. Add syrup, add the beaten egg.
Mix in flour, ginger, and spice and to this add soda melted in the milk.
Put into a well greased patty tin and bake for 1/2 to 3/4 hour.

Hilary Jenkin, Plymouth
(Taken from her mothers school exercise book and dates from early 1930's)

Ginger Cake Squares

Ingredients

8 oz (250g) Plain Flour
A good pinch of Salt
2 Level Tsp Ground Ginger
1 Level Tsp Bicarbonate of Soda
3 oz (100g) Dark Brown Soft Sugar
A little melted Fat
A rectangular tin measuring 7" by 11" by 1" deep.

5 oz (150g) Golden Syrup
5 oz (150g) Black Treacle
3 oz (100g) Margarine
2 Eggs (size 2 or 3)
1/2 Pint water

Method

Brush the tin with melted fat. Sift the flour with a pinch of salt, the ground ginger and the bicarbonate of soda. Put a fairly large pan on the scales and with a tablespoon in it check the weight. Spoon in the correct weight of golden syrup and black treacle. Take the pan off the scales and add the margarine and brown soft sugar and melt these together over a gentle heat. Beat the eggs and water and stir them into the mixture in the pan with the sifted ingredients. Mix thoroughly and pour the mixture into the tin. Bake the ginger cake in a moderate oven at about Gas mark 4, or 350°F, or 180°C for 40 to 45 minutes. Leave the ginger cake to cool in the tin before cutting into squares.

Note: *Ginger cake keeps well even without a freezer; put in a polythene bag or wrap it in foil.*

Brenda Parker, Cheltenham

Gingerbread Fruit Strudel

Ingredients

8 oz (225g) Gooseberries   2 oz (50g) Sultanas
3 oz (75g) Sugar   1 Tbsp Chopped Stem Ginger
1 oz (25g) Butter – melted   1 Tbsp Flaked Almonds
1 Tbsp Stem Ginger Syrup   1 Tsp Icing Sugar
3 oz (75g) Fresh White Breadcrumbs
 4 (14" x 8" / 35cm x 20cm) Sheets of Filo Pastry

Method

Place gooseberries, sultanas, 1 oz (25g) sugar and 2 tablespoonfuls of water
in a saucepan. Heat gently until sugar dissolves. Simmer for 5 - 10
minutes until gooseberries begin to soften. Remove from heat and mix in
the remaining sugar, breadcrumbs, chopped ginger and syrup.
Mixture should be thick but still wet.
Pre-heat oven to 190°C/375°F gas Mark 5.

Lightly grease a large baking sheet. Brush each sheet of filo pastry with
some of the melted butter and layer the sheets on top of each other.
Scatter gooseberry mixture on the pastry, leaving a 2.5cm/1" border all
round. Fold the 2 long sides over the filling and roll up the pastry,
beginning at one short end. Using a fish slice, transfer to baking sheet.
Brush with the remaining butter and sprinkle with Almonds.

Bake the strudel in the pre-heated oven for 40 minutes until golden brown
and crisp on the base. Transfer to serving plate and dust with icing sugar.
Serve hot/cold with cream, if liked.

Vera Banner, Ilfracombe

Sponge Parkin

Ingredients

8 oz Self Raisin Flour
1 - 2 Tsp of Ground Ginger
2 oz Lard
1 Level Tsp of Bicarbonate of Soda

4 oz Sugar
1 Cup of Boiled Milk
2 oz Margarine
1 Large Tbsp of Golden Syrup

Method

Mix all dry ingredients well. Cut fats into small pieces and add to flour etc.
Add syrup and milk last of all. Mix well to a soft consistency and bake at
Gas Mark 4 (Electric 350°F) for 1/2 to 3/4 hour.

Jean Horncastle, Westward Ho!

Ginger Cherry Loaf

Ingredients

9 oz Plain Flour
3 Tsp Ground Ginger
3 1/2 oz Crystallised Ginger
4 1/2 oz soft Brown Sugar

2 1/2 Tsp Baking Powder
4 1/2 oz Butter or Marge
5 oz Cherries
9 Tbsp Milk

Method

Sift dry ingredients, rub in fat. Stir in chopped ginger, cherries and sugar.
Add milk to make stiff dough.
Put in a lined 2lb Loaf Tin and cook at 350°F/180°C for 1 - 1 1/4 hours.
Serve sliced with butter.

Eileen Heasman, Crowborough

Caribbean Rum & Spice Cake

Ingredients

250g (9oz) Sultanas
250g (9oz) Raisins
140g (5oz) Chopped Dates
100g (3½oz) Glace Cherries, halved
140g (5oz) Plain Flour
5ml (1 Tsp) Ground Allspice
Finely Grated Rind & Juice of 1 Lime
55g (2oz) Brazil Nuts, Chopped
200g (7oz) Dark Muscovado Cane Sugar

4 Medium Eggs
90ml (6 Tbsp) Dark Rum
85g (3oz) Chopped Glace Ginger
200g (7oz) Unsalted Butter
2½ml (½Tsp) Grated Nutmeg
55g (2oz) Desiccated Coconut

Method

Place the sultanas, raisins, dates, cherries and ginger in a large bowl. Stir in the rum, lime zest and juice. Cover and leave to stand at room temperature overnight.

Preheat oven to 150° C, 300F°, Gas Mark 2.
Line a 23cm (9") tin with non-stick paper. Place an empty (400g) can in the centre, fill with baking beans and wrap with non-stick paper. Beat together the butter and sugar until light and fluffy. Gradually add the eggs beating hard after each addition.

Sift together the flour, allspice and nutmeg, then fold lightly and evenly into the mixture. Stir in the coconut and brazils with soaked fruit. Spoon the mixture into the tin and level the surface. Bake for 2 - 2¼ hours, or *until golden brown and firm.*

To test insert a skewer into the centre of the cake and it should come out clean. Cool the cake in the tin. Turn out, remove the paper and wrap in greaseproof paper and foil to store.

H. McMillan, Dingwall, Ross-shire

Aunt Peggys Ginger Cake

Ingredients

1/2lb Self Raising Flour
2oz Butter
1/2 Level Tsp Bicarbonate of Soda
2 Heaped Tsps of Ground Ginger
Milk to mix (about 3fl ozs)
Icing Sugar to decorate - *optional*

2oz Brown or White Sugar
1 Egg
1/4lb Golden Syrup
Pinch of Salt
3ozs Sultanas - *optional*

Method

Mix all dry ingredients together in bowl (plus sultanas). Heat syrup and butter slowly until melted (not over heat) Mix milk and beaten egg and add to mixed ingredients, then warm mixture also. Mix by hand to bind all together. Put into greased 8" sandwich tin or 1lb loaf tin.
Cook in mid oven at 180°C / 350°F for 25 mins. Ice when cold

Aunt Peggy

Ginger Buns

Ingredients

8oz Flour
4oz Margarine
2 Tablespoonfuls Ground Ginger
6 Tablespoonfuls Black Treacle (warmed)

4oz Sugar
2 Eggs

Method

Beat sugar and margarine, add beaten eggs. Mix dry ingredients thoroughly and add to the mixture. Then add the treacle. Drop into small greased moulds. Bake for 20 minutes at Gas 6 (400°F/200°C)

Mrs Peters, Barnstaple

Ginger Cake *(A wartime recipe I still use)*

Ingredients

1/2lb Self Raising Flour   4ozs Sugar
1 Tsp Bicarbonate of Soda   4ozs Marge
1 - 1^1/$_2$ Tsp Ginger (according to taste)
1 Dessertspoon of Syrup

Method

Rub fat into flour. Add sugar, ginger and syrup. Dissolve bicarbonate of soda in æ cup of hot water and mix it into dry ingredients.
Put into oven immediately at 375°F / 190°C. Bake for one hour.
(Fan ovens temp a little less and cooking time a little less)

Barbara Miles, Minehead

Ginger Cake

Ingredients

5 ozs Plain flour   1 Tsp Ground Ginger
1 Tsp Bicarbonate of Soda   1^1/$_2$ ozs Sugar
4 ozs Golden Syrup   4 Fl.Ozs Milk
2 ozs Margarine

Method

Grease and line a 7" square tin. Melt together sugar, margarine and syrup.
Add remaining dry ingredients. Lastly blend in the milk.
Pour into tin and bake at 160°C for about 30 minutes until firm to touch.
If kept a couple of days the top will go nice and sticky.

(I find this easy and ideal to cut into squares to sell at a fete or bazaar for charity, it makes a nice moist cake)

Carole Thorn, Alicante, Spain

Ginger Sponge Cake *(a simple honest ginger cake)*

Ingredients

175g/6ozs butter, softened   3 large eggs
2tsp ground ginger   2tbsp milk
175g/6ozs soft brown sugar or caster sugar
175g/6ozs self-raising flour sifted with

For the icing.
85g/3ozs softened butter   1 level sp ground ginger
85g/3ozs icing sugar, sifted   1tsp golden syrup

Method

Heat oven to 160/180°C, gas mark 4. Grease and line a 20cm/8" round tin. Put all the ingredients in a mixing bowl and beat them for a minute with a wooden spoon. Turn into tin and hollow centre slightly. Bake for between 75/90 minutes. Turn the cake out onto a wire rack and leave to cool.

To make the icing.

Put all the ingredients in a small saucepan and heat gently. When smooth remove the pan from the heat, allow to cool and, when icing is thick, pour it over the cake.

Tips

1 For the all-in-one mixing method to work, the butter must be softened to about room temperature. If the butter gets ever so slightly melted it will lighten the cake even more.

2 This amount of icing will cover the top and sides of the cake. To cover just the top of the cake use 2/3rds of the quantities.

3 When making icing, do not melt the butter before adding the other ingredients, it won't blend properly.

Mrs J R Ashdown, Torquay

Gingerbread Hollows

Ingredients

4oz margarine	12oz caster sugar
9oz self raising flour	1 large egg
2 level tsp ground ginger	

Method

Cream margarine and sugar, blend well and cream in the egg.
Stir in sieved flour and ginger. Work into a pliable dough, knead lightly and roll into balls about the size of a walnut. Place well apart on a greased baking sheet.
Bake (300°F, 150°C or regulo 2) for 25 minutes until just coloured and well puffed up. Cool on a wire rack.
(Can be frozen for 3 months.
I used granulated sugar: rolled out the dough and used cutters. The above mix will make 22 gingerbread men.)

Lesley Wright, Dorset

Moggy

This is one of my family's favourite recipes. It was given to me 35 years ago by a lady from the North East and it had been her mothers recipe - so it's quite old. It is basically a very sticky gingerbread. And gets better for keeping, (if you can keep any). Freezes well.

Ingredients

2 cups self raising flour	1 cup sugar
2oz butter	2oz margarine
3 large tbsp treacle	2 eggs
1 tsp bicarbonate of soda	
1 cup of 1/2 full cream milk and 1/2 water	
1 tsp ginger (11/2 for more ginger flavour)	

Method

Put all ingredients in a large pan except flour and eggs. Heat gently and as mixture begins to rise pour in to the flour gradually, beating all the time. Add the eggs and mix in. Pour into greased base lined baking tin (approx 10" x 6½")
Bake at 400°F for 5 - 10 minutes until middle begins to rise, then turn oven down to 325°F for ½ to ¾ hour.

Mrs Lesley Beck, Huddersfield

Ginger Shortcake

Ingredients

For Shortcake:

4 oz (114 grams) butter	2 oz (56 grams) caster sugar
5 oz (142 grams) plain flour	1 level tsp baking powder
1 level tsp powdered ginger	

For Icing:

2 oz (56 grams) butter	4 level tbsp sifted icing sugar
1 level tsp powdered ginger	3 level tsp golden syrup

Method

Shortcake
Cream butter and sugar until blended. Sift flour, baking powder and ginger together. Add to butter/sugar mixture and bind together.
Turn into 7½" (19cm) sandwich tin and flatten slightly in the centre.
Bake for 40 minutes at 335° F (175°C).

Icing.
Mix all ingredients in a saucepan over a low heat until blended.
Pour over shortcake in tin and leave to cool and set.

Rosemary Robinson, Brixworth

Christmas Gingerbread House

Ingredients

Cake
400g plain flour   2 tsp mixed spice
8 x 15ml spoons golden syrup   75g margarine
75g soft brown sugar   1 15ml bicarbonate of soda
2 x15ml spoons of water   1 egg plus another egg yolk

Butter Icing
100g butter or margarine   200g sifted icing sugar
2 x 5ml spoons lemon juice

American Frosting
175g caster sugar   1 egg white
2 x 15ml spoons hot water   1 pinch cream of tartar

Plus 10" square silver cake board, sweets to fill and decorate, cereal packet
cardboard to make templates.

Method

Make templates as on diagram.
Line two baking sheets with baking parchment. Set oven to 375°F / Gas
mark 5.
Sift the flour and spice into a bowl. Measure the golden syrup carefully and
put in a saucepan with the margarine and the sugar. Stir over a low heat
until the sugar has dissolved. Dissolve the bicarbonate of soda in the water
in a large bowl and then add the dry ingredients with the syrup mixture, egg
and egg yolk.
Mix together to form soft dough. Put half the dough in a polythene bag .
Roll out the other half to 6mm thick.
Cut out one of each roof, end, and side wall and arrange on a baking sheet.
Bake for 8 to 10 minutes or until risen and golden brown. Leave to cool
for a few minutes before transferring to a cooling rack.

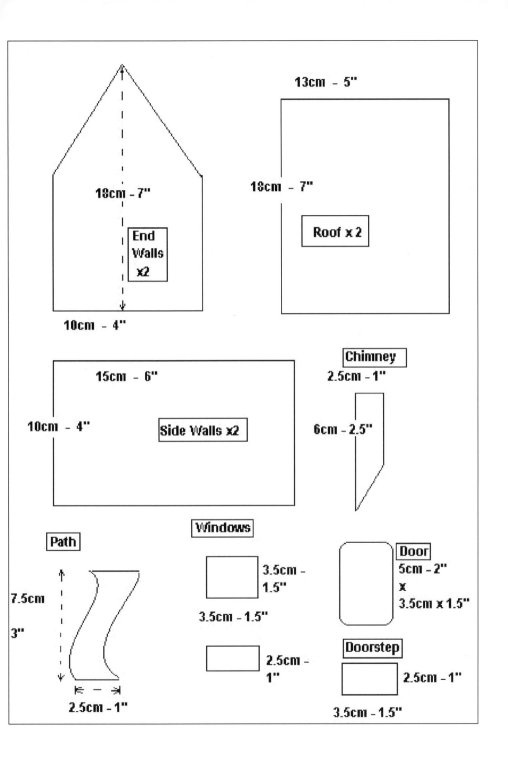

18cm – 7"

End Walls x2

10cm – 4"

13cm – 5"

18cm – 7"

Roof x 2

15cm – 6"

10cm – 4"

Side Walls x2

Chimney

2.5cm – 1"

6cm – 2.5"

Path

7.5cm

3"

2.5cm – 1"

Windows

3.5cm – 1.5"

3.5cm – 1.5"

2.5cm – 1"

Door

5cm – 2"
x
3.5cm x 1.5"

Doorstep

2.5cm – 1"

3.5cm – 1.5"

23

Knead and rollout the trimmings together with the other half of the dough and cut out another roof, end and side wall. Bake as before.
Knead together all the trimmings and cut out 2 doors, 2 doorsteps, 1 path, 4 square windows and 2 chimneypieces. Bake for 5 to 8 minutes and then allow to cool.

Make up butter icing, beat butter or margarine in bowl until soft. Beat in the icing sugar and lemon juice a little at a time until light and fluffy.
Make up on a cake board using butter icing to sandwich side and end pieces together, like a box. Fill with sweets - marshmallows are good.
Attach roof using plenty of icing to make secure. Leave the cake for about an hour before decorating. Arrange the outside pieces wherever they suit and secure with a little icing.

Make up the American frosting. Put all the ingredients in a heatproof bowl and place over a saucepan of hot, but not boiling water. Whisk until mixture thickens and soft peaks form when the whisk is lifted.
Remove the bowl form the saucepan and whisk until the mixture is cool.

Spread the frosting quickly over roof, tops of windows and doors. Pull points of icing down with a small knife to resemble snow. Trim the chimneypieces to size if needed, sandwich together with icing and place in position on roof using a cocktail stick to secure if required.

Cover top and sides of chimney with frosting. Arrange sweets around the windows, doors and roof. Stick the path on the cake board with icing
Spread the remaining frosting over the cake board and arrange as many sweets as you want. (We use maltesers, jelly babies, chocolate buttons and jazzies, jelly sweets etc.)

When it's time to eat the house, it's great fun to let the children, and adults, just dive in and demolish the whole thing - discovering the surprise inside. We made this for a children's Xmas party and it has become part of our family tradition.

Ella and Karen Clarke, Appledore

Ginger Polenta Cake

Ingredients

Cake

8oz butter, softened	8oz dark brown sugar
1 tbsp ground ginger	Pinch of salt
8oz fine polenta (cornmeal)	3oz ground almonds
1 level tsp baking powder	4 medium eggs

Topping
6 pieces stem ginger
2 tbsps ginger syrup (from stem ginger jar)
10^{1}/4" x 6^{1}/2" tray bake tin lined with baking parchment.

Method

Set the oven to warm gas mark 3 of 160℃. Beat the butter, sugar, ginger and salt together until light and fluffy, then beat in eggs. Fold in the polenta, ground almonds and baking powder. Spoon the mixture into the lined tin, and level the surface.

Bake the cake in the centre of the oven for 45 minutes to 1 hour, or until the cake is a light golden colour and it feels just firm to the touch in the centre. Remove from the oven and leave to cool for about 15 minutes.

Cut the stem ginger into long strips and scatter it over the cake. Then spoon the stem ginger syrup over. Leave the cake to cool completely and then cut into squares.

NOT SUITABLE FOR FREEZING

Grans Ginger Cake

Ingredients

2oz margarine	5oz caster sugar
9oz self raising flour	1 large egg
2 teaspoons ground ginger	7floz milk
1 teaspoon bicarbonate of soda	1 tbsp syrup
6 tablespoons boiling water	

Method

Put margarine, sugar in a large mixing bowl. Beat well, add the eggs and mix well. Add the syrup, self-raising flour, ginger and the milk. Mix together adding the bicarbonate of soda mixed with the boiling water. Mix well.
Place in a 7" square tin, greased and lined with greaseproof paper.
Bake at 350°F for 1 hour.

Molly Davies, Launceston

No Cook Swiss Roll Cake

Ingredients

1 Packet Ginger Biscuits	8oz Whipping Cream

Method

Whip half the cream and sandwich the biscuits together like a swiss roll.
Good to do the night before.
Whip remaining cream together and spread over and decorate before serving

Thelma Crook, Braunton

Grandmas Ginger Cake

Ingredients

6oz Butter	6oz Caster sugar
4 Eggs	10oz plain flour
1 Tsp Baking powder	1/4 Tsp Ground ginger
3oz Preserved ginger	1 Dessertspoon Black treacle
Little grated lemon rind	1 Dessertspoon Syrup
Tin size 6" –7"	*(from preserved ginger)*

Method

Beat butter and suger to a cream. Beat eggs and stir in gradually, beat well.
Mix baking powder and ground ginger to flour and stir into butter mixture.
Add grated lemon rind, chopped , very finely, preserved ginger, treacle and
syrup. Mix well, slowly with a wooden spoon. Turn into cake tin lined
with greased paper. Bake for 1 1/2 hours at 160°C, gas mk-3

Audrey Quinn, Braunton

Ginger Spice Cake (1934)

Ingredients

6oz Flour	3oz Butter
1/4 Tsp Bicarbonate of soda	1/2 Tsp Mixed spice
3oz Plain Chocolate	1 Tsp Ground ginger
3oz Icing sugar	10oz Sweet Almonds
2oz Citron peel	2oz Demerera sugar
2 Tbsp Milk	1/2 Teacup Treacle
Lined cake tin with buttered paper	

Method

Put flour, salt, spice and ginger through a sieve. Blanch and slice almonds.
Slice peel. Put sugar in a saucepan with treacle and butter. Stir until it
boils. Dissolve soda in milk. Stir in sugar etc. into flour, add milk. Mix
all well. Bake in very moderae oven for 1 1/2 hours. When cold cover with
chocolate icing.

Pam Siddons, Braunton

Biscuits

Anzac Biscuits with a Ginger Twist

Ingredients

1 cup flour	1 cup sugar
1 cup coconut	1 cup oats
4 oz butter	1 Tbsp syrup
1 Tsp bicarbonate of soda	1 Tbsp boiling water
3 Tsp ground ginger	pinch of salt

Method

Mix all the dry ingredients together and add to this the butter and syrup (which has already been melted together). Mix well, adding the boiling water last. Turn out the mixture onto a well floured surface and roll out to about 1/2" thickness.
Cut out the round biscuits and place on a baking tray. Cook for approximately 15 minutes at about 170°C. Once cooked leave to cool on a cooling rack. Biscuits will harden as they cook.

Jeanette Harding-Crook, Braunton

*This recipe was found just recently amongst a great Aunts belongings. .
It was her recipe for Anzac biscuits. I have added the ground ginger twist -
it works well together.*

Ginger Biscuits
(makes 36)

Ingredients

8 oz Plain Flour   Pinch of Salt
2 Tsp Ground Ginger   8 oz Demerara Sugar
4 oz Butter or Marge   1 Large Egg
1 Tbsp Milk   Almonds
1 Level tsp of Bicarbonate of Soda

Method

Sift flour and salt, add sugar. Rub in fat, add beaten egg and Bi-carb of soda
dissolved in milk. Mix well and knead on floured board, form into 36 balls.
Fatten slightly and place split almonds on each.
Bake for 30 minutes on gas mark 3

Mrs Edna Haffield, Essex

Ginger Oat Biscuits

Ingredients

4 oz Margarine   1 Dessert Spoon Syrup
3 oz Demerara Sugar   4oz Self Raising Flour
4 oz Oats   1 Rounded Tsp Ginger

Method

Melt margarine, sugar and syrup. Pour onto mixed dry ingredients, mix
well. Make into walnut sized and flatten slightly. Bake 10 - 15 minutes
until golden brown. Leave to cool on baking sheet for 10 minutes.

Brenda Briggs, Bude

Ginger Snaps

Ingredients

4 oz McDougalls Self-raising Flour	4 oz Sugar
4 oz Golden Syrup	4 oz Butter
Juice of 1/2 Lemon	1/4 oz Ground Ginger

Method

Put the butter and sugar, lemon juice and syrup into a saucepan and melt them slowly. Sift the flour and ginger together and add to the ingredients in the pan, warm gently but do not cook.

Remove from the heat and put teaspoonfuls of the mixture on to well-greased baking sheets three inches apart. (About five will go on an ordinary baking sheet.)

Put into a moderately hot oven, (Gas Mark 3 or 370°F Middle Shelf) and cook until they are nicely browned. Leave for a moment before removing them from the tin, then quickly take them off, turn them over, and loosely roll them round the handle of a wooden spoon. This process must be done rather quickly as they soon begin to crisp. Refill the tin with more mixture and proceed as directed.

Hilary Jenkins, Plymouth

Canadian Ginger Cookies

Ingredients

3/4 Cup of Shortening	1 Cup of Sugar
2 Cups sifted Self Raising Flour	1 Egg
2 Tsps of Baking Soda	1/4 Tsp of Salt
1 1/2 Tsps of Cinnamon	1 Tsp of Cloves
1/4 Cup Molasses (or Black Treacle)	2 Tsps of Ginger

N.B. 1 Cup = 12 Tablespoonfuls

Method

Cream shortening and sugar, add molasses and egg. Beat well. Add dry ingredients and blend well. Roll out on floured board. Cut into rounds (for crisp cookies roll thin). Bake at 375°F for 5 - 7 minutes on a greased cookie pan. Remove, put on rack to cool.

B. Girling, Hornsea, E. Yorks

Brandy Snaps *(Makes 18)*

Ingredients

1 level teaspoon of ground ginger   2oz butter
2oz caster sugar   2oz plain flour
2oz black treacle, a teaspoon of lemon juice

Method

Melt butter, sugar, black treacle and lemon juice together over a gentle heat. Add sieved flour and ginger, blend together.
Put teaspoonfuls of the mixture on well-greased baking trays, five inches apart. Bake 8 to 10 minutes in a moderately hot oven (350°F or Gas Mark 4) until a rich brown and well spread. Remove from the oven and leave to cool for a moment until they are easily lifted.
While still warm, wrap each one around a wooden spoon handle, working quickly. Allow to become firm before lifting onto a wire tray.
Store in an airtight tin.

Serve filled with fresh cream - at teatime or with coffee, or as a dessert for supper or dinner.

Mrs Margaret Cole, Peterborough

(Taken from The Lancashire Evening post in the 1960's)

Ginger Cookies

Ingredients

6 oz Caster Sugar
2 Tbsps of Milk
2 oz Corn flour
3 Tsps of Ground Ginger

6 oz Margarine
1 oz Plain flour
1 Tsp of Baking Powder

Method

Cream caster sugar and margarine, add all other ingredients together to a
soft dough. Form into a roll and cut off 1¹/4" slices. Put on baking sheet,
sprinkle with Demerara sugar and cook at 400°F/200°C, for 10 - 15
minutes.

Eileen Heasman, Crowborough

Ginger Stars

Ingredients

3oz (85g) Margarine
4oz (115g) Ground Ginger
Small pieces of Glace Ginger for decoration

2oz (60g) Golden Syrup

Method

Cream the marge and syrup together until blended. Sift the flour and ground
ginger together and fold into the creamed mixture.

Baking tray well greased. Bake in hot oven, 170° C or 340°F on gas mark
3. Middle shelf 12 - 15 minutes until Golden Brown.

Piped with star piping gun or inn thin fingers and sandwiched together with
ginger jam or butter cream - (4oz butter & 6oz icing sugar)

Mrs M J Cocks

Ginger Nuts

Ingredients

6ozs self raising flour
1 1/2 ozs margarine
1 level tsp mixed spice
1/4 tsp bi-carbonate of soda
1 tsp milk

2 tbsps syrup
1 tbsp sugar
1 level tsp of ground ginger
Pinch of salt

Method

Mix flour, spice, salt and ginger together. Put sugar, syrup and fat into a saucepan and melt over a gentle heat without making too hot.
Stir bi-carb into this mixture.
Pour into the dry ingredients with the milk and mix to a stiff dough.
Roll teaspoons of the mixture into balls, put on a flat greased tin and flatten each round down to a biscuit shape.
Bake in a moderate oven about 15 minutes or until golden brown.

Mrs M Prescott

Cornish Fairings

Ingredients

2 tbsps syrup
8oz caster Sugar
2 level tsps ground ginger
2 level tsps bicarbonate of soda

8oz block of margarine
10oz plain flour
1/2 level tsp salt

Method

Melt together syrup, marge and sugar in a saucepan. Stir in bicarbonate of soda, (froths up). Sift together flour, ginger and salt. Mix together well and form into balls. Place on a greased baking sheet allowing plenty of room for spreading. Cook for 10 - 15 minutes in a pre-heated oven, 160°C until golden brown.

Ginger Shortcake *(nice and chewy)*

Ingredients

8oz (250g) self raising flour)	Sift into
2 tsp ginger)	bowl

4oz (125g) sugar)	Melt in
4oz (125g) margarine)	a small
1 tbsp golden syrup)	saucepan

Method

Add melted mixture to flour mixture, mix and knead. Spread evenly into greased 8" (20cm) square tin. Bake slowly (150°C, gas 3) for 30 - 40 minutes until just shrinking from sides of tin (it will firm up as it cools). Ice whilst hot with thin icing made from 4oz (125g) icing sugar, $1/2$ - 1 tsp ginger and a little water. Decorate with chopped stem ginger if liked and cut into squares/fingers.

Sue Lucas, Fishponds, Bristol

Gingerbread People

Ingredients

50g butter or hard block margarine	100g golden syrup
50g golden caster sugar	200g self-raising flour
1 heaped teaspoon ground ginger	

For decoration

Icing pens
Chocolate buttons

Method

Pre-heat oven to 180°C, 350°F, Gas mark 4). Put the butter, sugar and syrup in the saucepan. Heat it gently until the sugar has dissolved, do not allow the mixture to boil. Remove the pan from the heat. Stir in all the flour and ginger until you have a smooth, manageable, stiff dough. Put the mixture in a bowl and put it aside to cool for 30 minutes. Meanwhile lightly grease your baking sheet.

Take the cooled dough out of the bowl. Sprinkle some flour on a surface and roll out until it's about 1/2cm thick. Use your cutters to cut out your biscuits. If you can't get hold of any cutters cut the shapes out of card and use them as templates.

Lift the cut out figures gently using a fish knife and place them on the baking tin. Put them in the oven for ten minutes. When the figures are golden and slightly risen remove from the oven. Let them cool for 5 minutes on the baking tin before placing them on a cooling rack. Decorate the figures with icing pens and chocolate buttons when they are completely cold.

Granny Ellen's Ginger Biscuit

Ingredients

8oz self raising flour   4oz butter/ margarine
3oz sugar   3 tsp ginger
4oz golden syrup

Method

Put flour, ginger and sugar in a bowl and mix together. Heat syrup and butter and melt until soft, do not boil. Add to bowl and mix with wooden spoon. Take small amount and roll into a ball and press flat on a greased tray. Cook on medium heat in middle of oven for 10 minutes.

Jan Dixon, Bideford

Gingerbread Flowers *(makes 25 biscuits)*

Ingredients

350g (12oz) plain flour
2 tbsps golden syrup
1/2 tsp ground cinnamon
100g (4oz) chilled butter or margarine
175g (6oz) light Muscovado sugar
writing icing & a flower shaped cookie cutter

1 1/2 tsps ground ginger
1 medium egg
1 tsp bicarbonate of soda

Method

Pre-heat oven to 180°C, 350°F, Gas mark 4) Use a paper towel to wipe a little oil over two baking trays. Use a sieve to sift the flour into a large mixing bowl. Sift the ginger, cinnamon and bicarbonate of soda into the bowl too. Cut the butter or margarine into chunks and stir it in so that it is coated with flour.

Use your fingertips to rub the chunks of butter or margarine into the flour, until the mixture looks like fine breadcrumbs. Then stir in the sugar. Break the egg into a small bowl and beat it in. Add the eggy mixture to the flour, then mix everything together, until you have a smooth dough. Holding the bowl in one hand use your other hand to squeeze the mixture together. Use a blunt knife to cut the dough in half.

Sprinkle a little flour onto a clean work surface and put one piece of the dough onto it. Then roll out the dough until it is about 5mm (1/4") thick. Use a flower shaped cookie cutter to cut out lots of flower shapes from the dough. Use a spatula to lift the shapes onto the baking trays. Roll out the other half of the dough and cut more flower shapes from it. Squeeze the scraps of dough together to make a ball and roll it out to cut more shapes.

Put the biscuits into your oven and bake them for 12 - 15 minutes until they are dark golden. Leave the biscuits on the trays for five minutes to cool. Use a spatula to lift the biscuits onto a wire rack.
When they are cold draw patterns on them with writing icing, or make your own icing to pipe on.

Jenny Walker, Bideford

Ginger Shortcake

Ingredients

Shortcake

4oz butter   2oz caster sugar
5oz plain flour   1 level tsp baking powder
1 level tsp ground ginger

Icing

4 level tbsps sifted icing sugar   2oz butter
1 level tsp ground ginger   3 level tsps golden syrup

Method

Beat the butter to a soft cream then beat in the caster sugar - they must be very well beaten together. Sift the flour, baking powder and the ground ginger, then mix this into the creamed mixture.

Grease the tin and spread the mixture on it. Bake in a very moderate oven, about gas mark 3 or 335°F for about 40 minutes. While the shortcake is still hot in the tin put the ingredients for the icing into a saucepan and melt them together. Pour this mixture over the top of the shortcake and spread it evenly.

 Leave the shortcake in the tin and cut into pieces while still warm. When cold ease the slices out with a knife.
Mark a curved pattern on each slice with a fork

Margaret and Vince Peppard, Washford, Somerset

Found recipe in Woman's Weekly magazine the week we got married 24/3/62. Has remained a firm favourite since.

Savouries

Fresh Vietnamese Soup

Ingredients

4 Cups of Chicken Stock (from cubes, liquid or home made)
1 Tbsp of White Vinegar   1 Tsp of Ground Ginger
Large handful of Rice Noodles   1 Tbsp of White Sugar
Large handful of Watercress chopped roughly into 1 or 2 inch pieces.
Large handful of white mushrooms sliced.

Method

Heat Chicken Stock. Add vinegar, ginger and sugar. Add rice noodles and cook for approx 1 minute swirling with a fork. Add a little salt if required. Just before serving add remaining ingredients: watercress and mushrooms. Serve and enjoy.

Elizabeth Dinsmor, Quebec

Ginger and Honey Pork Chop

Ingredients

2 Tbsps of Olive Oil   Seasoning
Generous pinch of Ground Ginger   1 Pork Chop
1 Tablespoonful of Honey

Method

Heat all in frying pan. Nick the chop all the way round he fat edge to prevent it from curling. Season chop and fry for 2 minutes.
Turn chop and sprinkle with ginger and honey. Cook for another 2 minutes, turn again and reduce heat. Cook until meat is tender.

Jean Barbour, Taunton

Beef Strips with Orange and Ginger *(Serves 4)*

Ingredients

450g (1lb) Beef Strips
15ml (1tbsp) Soy Sauce
2¹/₂ cm (1") Root Ginger
1 Carrot

1 Orange
5ml (1 tsp) Corn flour
10ml (2tsp) Sesame Oil
2 Spring Onions

Method

Place beef strips in a bowl: sprinkle over the rind and juice of the orange.
Leave to marinate for at least 30 minutes. Drain the liquid and set aside,
then mix the meat with soy sauce, corn flour and root ginger.
Heat sesame oil in a wok or large frying pan and add the beef.
Stir-fry for 1 minute, add 1 carrot, cut into small strips and stir-fry for a
further 2 - 3 minutes. Stir in 2 sliced spring onions and the reserved liquid,
then boil, stirring, until thickened. Serve with egg noodles.

Amanda Lovelock, Bideford, Devon

Beef Casserole with Rhubarb & Ginger

Ingredients

8oz (250gm) Stewing Steak and flour to coat
1 medium onion
1 tin rhubarb
Salt, pepper, sugar to taste

1oz (25gm) olive oil
1 tsp of dry ginger
1 pint stock or water

Method

Heat olive oil. Dust meat with flour, salt and pepper. Gently fry coated
meat until brown. Sauté chopped onion. Put meat, onion and rhubarb into
dish. Sprinkle with ginger. Add stock or water. Cover and cook for 30 - 40
minutes in moderate oven, gas mark 6 or 350°C, until meat is tender.
Check seasoning (adding sugar if necessary). Serve with boiled potatoes,
rice or pasta

Mrs Kathleen M Drinkwater, Manchester

Gingered Pork *(serves 4 - 6 depending on appetite)*

Ingredients

2lbs Lean Pork	1oz Flour
1 1/2 teaspoonfuls salt	Ground Black Pepper
2 tsps Ground Ginger	12oz Carrots
4 tbsps oil	

Rice

12oz Long Grain Rice	1oz Butter
1 Large Onion, chopped	2oz Sultanas
2oz Flaked Almonds	

Sauce

1/4 teaspoonful Tabasco	14oz Can of Tomatoes
2 tbsps Worcester Sauce	4 tbsps Brown Sugar
4 tbsps Vinegar	2 Cloves Garlic, crushed
1 Bay Leaf	1 Bunch Spring Onions

Method

Oven Gas Mark 3, 325°F, 170°C. Cut the meat into thin strips about 3" long and 1/2" wide. Mix flour, seasoning and ground ginger and coat meat. Peel carrots, slice lengthways, then cut slices into matchsticks. Heat oil in a large ovenproof pan and fry the pork in batches until brown. Add the carrots.

Combine all the sauce ingredients and pour over the meat. Cover and cook in the oven for 2 - 3 hours until the meat is tender. Make spring onion tassels by slicing lengthways through the green part of the onion and placing in cold water for about an hour.

Cook the rice for 11 minutes in plenty of boiling water and then drain. Cook the onion in butter and mix in the almonds, sultanas and rice. Arrange on a serving dish and garnish with the spring onions.

Mrs Rossiter, Sidmouth

Ginger & Garlic Brussels Sprouts

Ingredients

$1/2$ tbsp finely chopped garlic $1/2$ tbsp grated fresh root ginger
1 tsp grated lemon zest $3/4$ tsp fennel seeds
1lb (454g) Brussel Sprouts, ends trimmed
12 fl oz (375ml) chicken stock or water
Salt & freshly ground black pepper

Method

Cut the stems of the sprouts and remove any bruised leaves. Cut the
sprouts in half and then into very thin strips. Bring 8 fl oz (250ml) of the
stock or water to the boil in a large saucepan. Reduce to a simmer and add
the sprouts, garlic, ginger and lemon zest.
Cook uncovered over a high heat, stirring often, for about 5 minutes or
until the sprouts are tender. Add the reserved stock if they are getting too
dry. Stir in the fennel seeds, salt and pepper.

*This dish works well as part of a collection of Chinese entrees or as an
accompaniment to a main course.*

Judy Fetherston, Norwich

Ginger Pumpkin Puree *(serves 6)*

Ingredients

2lb Prepared pumpkin   2 - 3 oz butter
2 heaped tsp ground ginger   Salt and plenty of black pepper

Method

Peel pumpkin - remove centre and seeds. Cook in lidded saucepan half
filled with water, takes 20 - 30 minutes to soften completely.
Drain and mash - return to gentle heat, stir in butter, ginger and
seasonings. Let moisture dry out on a mild heat, pile on to a dish and serve
hot.

Jeanne Clarke

Apple Cassoulet

A sauce to serve with meat/vegetable dishes or quorn. Serves 4)

Ingredients

8 small onions, peeled
1 tbsp brown sugar
2 x 410g tins cannellini beans
2 red skinned apples, complete with the skin, cored and sliced.
2.5cm (1") fresh ginger, peeled and coarsely grated.
310ml (110fl.oz) unsweetened apple juice
Salt and freshly ground black pepper.

50g (2oz) butter
1 level tsp corn flour
$1/2$ level tsp mustard powder

Method

You will need one large lidded frying pan or large casserole dish. In the pan, or dish, melt half the butter, add apple slices and cook turning once until translucent. Transfer to a plate. Add remaining butter and toss in onions. Cook for 10 minutes. Sprinkle with sugar half way through to gain colour and sweet flavour.
Drain and rinse beans under cold water. Drain thoroughly and add to onions, stir well. In a small bowl, combine corn flour, ginger, mustard, apple juice and good seasoning of pepper. Blend to dissolve corn flour. Stir mixture into pan. Bring to a simmer and stir until sauce has thickened. Taste, adjust seasoning. Cover and simmer 10 minutes, add apple slices and simmer 5 minutes before serving.

Sally Jubb, Fareham, Hants

CALDEIRADA DE PEIXE   Fishermans Stew

Ingredients

1kg fish - Eels, swordfish, tuna, sardines, skate etc. etc. may be used. My favourite is CHOCO, Cuttlefish

500g potatoes   1kg tomatoes
750kg onions   Olive oil
1 glass of white wine   Coriander leaves & Parsley
Sliced carrot and green pepper may also be added
Bay leaves, salt, paprika, marjoram, garlic and Ginger to taste.
Parsley

Method

In a large stew pot place alternate layers of prepared fish, finely sliced onions, medium sliced potatoes and diced tomatoes. Add seasonings, wine, olive oil. Simmer on low fire with lid on. Some water may be added but it's not usually necessary if ingredients are fresh.
Cook until everything is well done, about 1 hour. Shake the pot a few times during cooking rather than stirring the stew.

As this is a traditional recipe - ingredients and instructions, like grandmothers, vary, but any version tastes delicious.

Portugal

Desserts

Ginger Pudding   *(serves 4)*

Ingredients

6 oz Plain Flour	2 Tbsps Sugar
2 Tsps Ground Ginger	1 oz Margarine
2 Tsps Bicarbonate of Soda	$1/2$ Pint Milk
3 oz Sultanas or Dates (chopped)	

Method

Sift flour, soda and ginger into a bowl. Add the sugar and sultanas (or dates). Boil milk and margarine then pour into bowl and mix well. Grease a 2 pint basin and put in the mixture, cover with greaseproof paper. Steam for $1 1/2$ hours. Serve with custard or sweet sauce.

Enid Dunscombe, Cardiff City

Ginger Cream

Ingredients

$1/4$ lb Crystallised Ginger	$1/4$ Pint Whipping Cream
Sugar	

Method

Chop crystallised ginger into small pieces. Whip cream and add ginger and sugar to taste. Put into dishes and serve with Ginger Snaps.

Jean Horncastle, Westward Ho!

Mango and Ginger Trifle *(serves 10)*

Ingredients

1 Jamaica Ginger Cake	45ml (3 tbsp) Dark Rum
2 Bananas, thickly sliced	1 x 200ml tub Crème Fraiche
1 x 400g carton of Fresh Custard	2 x 125g tubs Vanilla Yoghurt

1 x 410g can of Mango Slices, drained and chopped.
2 pieces Stem Ginger (in syrup), cut into thin sticks
5g (1 oz) Pistachio Nuts, chopped (optional)

Method

Slice the cake and arrange in the base of a large glass serving dish. Sprinkle over the Rum, then place the mangoes and bananas evenly on top. Spoon custard over the fruit. Blend yoghurt and crème fraiche and swirl over the custard. Decorate with the ginger and pistachios, cover and chill.

Joan Cope, Wokingham

Ginger Candy *(about 54 pieces)*

Ingredients

1lb Soft Brown Sugar	1/4 Pint (125ml) Water
2 Level Tsps Ground Ginger	1oz Butter
2oz Golden Syrup	

Method

Well butter or oil a tin measuring 8" square. Put all ingredients into a large heavy saucepan. Heat slowly, stirring all the time, until sugar dissolves and butter melts. Bring to boil and cover with lid, boil for 2 minutes then uncover. Continue to boil steadily, stirring once or twice until a little of the mixture forms a soft ball when dropped into cold water. Cool for 5 minutes then beat briskly until mixture becomes cloudy. Spread into prepared tin and cut into squares when cold and set.

Carol Halliday, Edgbaston

Gingerbread Upside Down Pudding

Ingredients

Topping:
15g / 1/2 oz Butter	4 Ripe Pears
15ml / 1tbsp Golden Syrup	9 Walnut Halves

Sponge:
115g / 4oz Plain Flour	5ml / 1tsp Ground Ginger
2 1/2ml / 1/2 tsp Bicarbonate of Soda	60ml / 4tbsp Milk
5ml / 1tsp Ground Cinnamon	45ml / 3tbsp Sunflower Oil
115g / 4oz Dark Marmalade	60ml / 4tbsp Golden Syrup
1 Egg	

Method

Preheat oven 180°C/350°F Gas Mark 4. Put butter, syrup in a pan, heat gently stirring until melted. Pour into 23cm / 9" round deep cake tin to cover base. Peel pear thinly, half lengthways. Scoop out core, place walnut into cavity and arrange cut side down. Sieve flour, soda, ginger and cinnamon into bowl.
In a separate bowl beat eggs, sugar, syrup, milk, and oil thoroughly. Make a well in flour and add the liquid mixture. Beat well to make a smooth batter. Pour batter mix over pears and bake 35 - 40 minutes until firm to touch. To serve - Greek Yoghurt or Custard

Helena Turner, Launceston

Ginger and Pear Trifle

Dice a Ginger Cake (i.e. McVities)
Place in bottom of glass dish. Pour a tin (Medium size) of Pears over cake. (– do not use all the juice) Pour custard over Pears
Leave to set. Decorate with pieces of stem ginger. Serve.

Joyce Curtis, Sleaford, Lincolnshire

Apricot (or Peach) Brown Betty

Ingredients

15 oz Tin of Apricot Halves	1 Tsp of Ground Ginger
4ozs Butter	2ozs Brown Sugar
4ozs Fine Oatmeal	4ozs Brown Bread Crumbs

Method

Drain apricots and add ginger. Melt butter, stir in sugar, oatmeal and breadcrumbs. Place half apricots on bottom of ovenproof dish. Place half oatmeal mixture on top, add rest of apricots and finish off with remaining oatmeal mixture. Cook at 350°F, (Gas Mark 4, Fan Oven 160°C) for approx 25 minutes. Serve warm or cold. Yummy! Will freeze.

Nola Smith, Abingdon

Spiced Pear Trifle *(serves 4)*

Ingredients.

225g (8oz) ginger cake, broken into largish pieces.

200g (7oz) tinned pears	90ml (3fl.oz) dark rum
300ml (10fl.oz) cold custard sauce	1 teaspoon icing sugar
150ml (5fl.oz) double cream, whipped	

Toast flaked almonds to decorate

Method

Place half the ginger cake pieces in the bottom of a large serving bowl (preferably glass).Drain the pears, reserving 60ml (2fl.oz) of the juice. Mix the rum with the reserved pear juice and sprinkle half over the cake in the bowl.
Cut the pears into large chunks and place on top of the cake. Cover with the remaining pieces of cake and pour over the remaining rum. Pour the custard over the top.
In another bowl whip the cream together with the icing sugar then spoon over. To serve - decorate with the toasted almonds.

Doreen Hemsworth, Essex

Maraschino and Ginger Mousse

Ingredients

3oz Maraschino cherries, chopped	3/4 pint of milk
1 1/2 level tsps corn flour	3 level tbsps sugar
2 large eggs separated	4 level tsps gelatine
3 tbsps cold water	3oz sultanas
3 tbsps syrup from cherry jar	1/4 pint double cream

1 1/2 oz crystallised ginger or ginger flavoured pieces chopped
(I use stem ginger in syrup then add a little syrup to the mixture)

Method

Blend the corn flour to a smooth paste with a little of the milk. Bring the rest to the boil then pour it on the corn flour stirring all the while. Return the sauce to the pan and boil for one minute, stirring continuously. Remove pan from heat, stir in the sugar then the egg yolks. Sprinkle the gelatine over the water in a small basin and leave to soak for a minute or so. When spongy stir it into the sauce until it has dissolved.

Stir in the maraschino cherries, syrup, sultanas and ginger and leave in a cool place to half set. When the fruit is on the point of setting, whisk the egg whites until stiff but silky, and the cream until fairly thick. Fold the egg whites and cream into the setting cherry mixture then pour into a wetted jelly mould or dish. Leave in a cool place. When set, turn it out and decorate with a few extra cherries on cocktail sticks.

A delicious Christmas treat.

Paulette Griffiths

Ginger Pudding *(serves 6)*

Ingredients

200g (7oz) plain flour	5ml (1tsp) ground ginger
Pinch of salt	100g (4oz) shredded suet
5ml (1tsp) bicarbonate of soda	1 egg - beaten
75g (3oz) caster sugar	15ml (3tsp) black treacle
50 - 100ml (2 - 3½ fl oz) milk	

Method

Grease a 1 litre (1¾ pint) pudding dish. Prepare a steamer or half fill a large saucepan with water and bring to boil. Sift flour, ginger, salt and bicarbonate of soda into a mixing bowl. Add sugar, suet and mix lightly.

In a second bowl beat the treacle and egg with 50ml (2 fl oz) of the milk. Stir the liquid mixture into the dry mixture adding more milk if necessary to give a soft dropping consistency. Spoon the mixture into the prepared basin, cover with greaseproof paper and foil secured with string.

Put into steamer, or stand it on a plate in the pan of boiling water. The water should come half way up the side the basin. Cover pan tightly and steam gently for 1¾ - 2 hours Serve with Ginger Syrup. *(See next recipe)*

Jenny Walker, Bideford

Ginger Syrup Sauce *(Makes about 300ml / 1/2 pint)*

Ingredients

Strip of lemon rind   Piece of fresh root ginger
100g (4oz) soft light brown sugar   5ml (1tsp) lemon juice
100g (4oz) golden syrup or honey   10ml (2 tsp) arrowroot
125ml (4oz) ginger syrup - (i.e. jar preserved)
15ml (1 tblsp) preserved ginger - chopped
2.5 ml (1/2 tsp) ground ginger

Method

Put lemon rind, root ginger and syrup into a saucepan.
Add 4oz water and heat to boiling point. Lower heat and simmer for 15
minutes. Remove the lemon rind and root ginger. Then add the brown sugar
and syrup or honey. Bring to the boil for 5 minutes, stir in the lemon
juice.
In a cup mix the arrowroot and ground ginger with a little cold water until
smooth. Stir the arrowroot mixture into the hot liquid. Heat gently until
liquid thickens, stirring all the time. Add the preserved ginger to the sauce
and simmer for 2 - 3 minutes.
Serve hot.

Jenny Walker, Bideford

Ginger and Honey Ice Cream   *(makes about a litre)*

Ingredients

284ml (10oz) Double Cream   4 large eggs
115g (4oz) caster sugar   1 tsp vanilla essence
1 level tbsp ground ginger

Method

Take three bowls, 1 mixing bowl and two smaller ones.
Into bowl 1, (mixing bowl) put the double cream
Into bowl 2 put the whites of 4 eggs.
Into bowl 3 put the egg yolks, the caster sugar and the vanilla essence.

Using a hand whisk. Whisk the egg whites (bowl 2) until they are quite
stiff. Then mix the cream (mixing bowl) until stiff. Then whisk (bowl 3)
– these ingredients will only thicken a little.
Into bowl 3 add the ground ginger and the honey and whisk to thoroughly
mix. Take bowl 3 and add to mixture bowl. Mix well, then take bowl 2
and add to mixture bowl.
Stir the egg whites in thoroughly, using a metal spoon. Put mixture in a
plastic container and freeze.
(The ginger and honey can be adjusted to your personal taste when you
make your next Ice Cream)

Christine Higgins, Hartland

Thirty foot Knitted Christmas Tree at Atlantic Village, Bideford, winter 2005/2006

Original drawing used to illustrate and promote the project

A selection of knitting received

Promoting the project at Wonderwool Wales May 2007

These knitted cakes look good enough to eat

Tom from Blackdog helping to knit the giant rug for the house with 5foot needles

Mrs. T. teaching her grand-daughters to knit during National Knitting week

A selection of knitting received from Oreston Methodist Church, Plymouth

Work in progress – the house beginning to take shape

A section of the roof being sewn together - over a thousand roof tiles and even more sweets!

The first day on display, 28th June 2007, with a happy cat sleeping on the bed.

The Gingerbread Man admiring his new home

Preserved Stem Ginger & Butterbean Ice Cream

Ingredients

225kg tin of butter beans, drained, uncooked
6 pieces of preserved stem ginger (chopped into 1/4" cubes)
1 tbsp of stem ginger syrup or golden syrup
400ml milk, preferably full fat
280ml double cream   100ml natural yoghurt
100g caster sugar   20g dark Muscovado sugar
5 egg yolks   1 tsp vanilla extract
A loaf tin or plastic tub, about 15 x 20 x 10cm deep.

Method

Place the beans, milk, egg yolks, all the sugar and vanilla extract in a saucepan. Heat until nearly boiling and slightly thickened. Then put the mixture in a blender and blitz until smooth. Sieve the bean mixture to remove any butter bean skins and leave to cool. Place the mixture in the freezer until just firm to touch.

In the meantime whip the double cream until fluffy but not quite thick and place in the fridge to chill. Line the loaf tin with cling film if not using a plastic container. Pour the bean mixture, double cream, yoghurt, stem ginger and ginger syrup into a bowl and fold the mixture until everything is stirred in. Pour this mix into the tin/tub and place in the freezer until barely firm again.

Remove from the freezer and use a hand whisk to mix. Place back in the freezer until ready to eat.

Sarah May Johnson, London

Jams

Marrow Marmalade with Ginger

Ingredients

4lbs Marrow	2lbs Apples
4lbs Sugar	1oz Ground Ginger
Rind and Juice of 2 Lemons	

Method

Peel Marrow and remove seed. Cut into small pieces (approx 1" and 2").
Peel and juice apples. Add ginger and juice and finely sliced rind of the
lemons. Put all ingredients in a large pan. Bring to the boil and simmer for
approximately 1 hour. Pour into sterilised warm jars and seal.
Enjoy

Joan Coils, Coventry

Ginger Marmalade

Ingredients

$1/2$g (1lb) Cooking Apples	7 g ($1/4$oz) Root Ginger
250ml ($1/2$ pint) Water	$1/2$ Kg (1lb) Preserving Sugar
100g (4oz) Preserved Ginger finely chopped	

Method

Wash apples (do not peel). Slice them and put in a large glass bowl.
Bruise the ginger, tie in muslin and put in with apple.
Add water. Cover with film and cook for 10 minutes on 100% power in a
micro-wave - remove ginger. Press apples through a sieve to extract juice
(approx 500ml or 1pint). Add sugar and preserved ginger, cook for 25
minutes on 100% power stirring every 5 minutes. Cool for 20 - 30
minutes before pouring into jars.

Mrs Petch, Barnstaple

Ginger Apple Preserve

Ingredients

4lb Apples
2 Lemons (Rind and Juice)
2 tsps ground ginger

1 Pint water
3lb Sugar
4oz Preserved ginger

Method

Peel, core and cut up apples. Place in a preserving pan with lemon juice, grated peel, water and ground ginger. Cook until tender. Add sugar and chopped preserved ginger. Stir until sugar dissolves then boil until setting point reached.

Jeanne Clarke

Rhubarb and Ginger Jam   *(makes about 1.4Kg - 3lb)*

Ingredients

1.1Kg (2^{1}/2lb) sugar
25g (1oz) fresh root ginger
100g (4oz) preserved or crystallised ginger, chopped
1.1Kg (2^{1}/2lb) trimmed rhubarb, chopped

Juice of 2 lemons

Method

Put the rhubarb in a large bowl in alternate layers with the sugar and lemon juice, cover and leave overnight.
Next day, bruise the root ginger slightly, with a weight or rolling pin, and tie it in a piece of muslin. Put the rhubarb mixture into a preserving pan with the muslin bag, bring to the boil and boil rapidly for 15 minutes. Remove the muslin bag; add the preserved or crystallised ginger and boil it for a further 5 minutes or until the rhubarb is clear. Test for a set and, when setting point is reached, take the pan off the heat and skim the surface with a slotted spoon. Pot and cover the jam.

Christine Higgins, Hartland

Beverages

Peach Apple and Ginger Fizz

Ingredients

2 Medium Peaches peeled, stoned and chopped
12 ml (4 fl oz) Apple Juice - Chilled
600 ml (1 pint) Ginger Ale - Chilled
Crushed Ice
Apple Slices to decorate - optional

Method

Place peaches and apple juice in a blender and process until smooth. With machine still running add ginger ale.
Place crushed ice in each of 4 tumblers. Pour in fizzy drink. Decorate with an apple slice if required. Serve immediately whilst still frothing.

Dee King, Looe, Cornwall

Ginger Beer

Ingredients

5 Quarts of Boiling Water
1 oz Whole Ginger (Bruised)
1/4oz Cream of Tartar

1 1/4 lbs Sugar
2 Lemons
1 Good Tbsp of Brewers Yeast

Method

Remove the rind of the lemons as thinly as possible. Strip off every particle of the white pith and cut the lemons into thin slices removing the pips.
Put the sliced lemon into an earthenware bowl with the sugar, ginger and cream of tartar and pour in the boiling water.
Allow it to stand until milk warm then stir in the yeast and let the bowl remain in a moderately warm place for 24 hours. Skim the yeast off the top. Strain the ginger beer carefully from the sediment.
Bottle, tie the corks down securely and in 2 days it will be ready to drink.

Margaret Lovelock, Bideford

Peach Apple and Ginger Fizz

Ingredients

2 Medium Peaches peeled, stoned and chopped
12 ml (4 fl oz) Apple Juice - Chilled
600 ml (1 pint) Ginger Ale - Chilled
Crushed Ice
Apple Slices to decorate - optional

Method

Place peaches and apple juice in a blender and process until smooth. With
machine still running add ginger ale.
Place crushed ice in each of 4 tumblers. Pour in fizzy drink. Decorate with
an apple slice if required. Serve immediately whilst still frothing.

Dee King, Looe, Cornwall

Ginger Beer

Ingredients

5 Quarts of Boiling Water   1 1/4 lbs Sugar
1 oz Whole Ginger (Bruised)   2 Lemons
1/4oz Cream of Tartar   1 Good Tbsp of Brewers Yeast

Method

Remove the rind of the lemons as thinly as possible. Strip off every
particle of the white pith and cut the lemons into thin slices removing the
pips.
Put the sliced lemon into an earthenware bowl with the sugar, ginger and
cream of tartar and pour in the boiling water.
Allow it to stand until milk warm then stir in the yeast and let the bowl
remain in a moderately warm place for 24 hours. Skim the yeast off the
top. Strain the ginger beer carefully from the sediment.
Bottle, tie the corks down securely and in 2 days it will be ready to drink.

Margaret Lovelock, Bideford

Ginger and Lemon Tea *(2 pints)*

Ingredients

2 pints water   Juice and rind of lemon
3ozs freshly grated ginger   4 tbsp honey
Thin slices of lemon - garnish

Method

Boil water, remove from heat and add lemon juice, lemon slices and ginger.
Steep for 20 minutes. Stir in honey, strain and chill. Serve on ice with
freshly sliced lemon

Jeanne Clarke

Traditional Spiced Mulled Wine *(makes 24 glasses)*

Ingredients

1 1/2 litres of water   1 orange, studded with 10 cloves
2 oranges and 2 lemons sliced   6 tablespoons sugar or honey
5cm cinnamon stick   2 tablespoons fruit liqueur
2 teaspoons finely grated fresh root ginger
2 bottles of medium or full bodied red wine

Method

Put all ingredients into a large saucepan.
Heat gently for 20 minutes DO NOT BOIL
Stir to ensure sugar dissolved. Keep warm over a low heat. Use a ladle to
serve.

Herbal Ginger Brew

Ingredients

Ginger Syrup:
1/2 cup peeled and sliced fresh ginger
1 cup purified water
1/2 cup pure maple syrup

1 cup carbonated mineral water
1 tablespoon fresh squeezed lemon juice
1 strip lemon peel

Method

To make the ginger syrup combine the sliced ginger and water and simmer for 30 minutes. Cool slightly, then strain. Add the maple syrup and stir to mix. You should have about a cup of syrup.

Stir 2 tablespoons of the syrup into the carbonated water until thoroughly mixed; refrigerate the remainder of the syrup for later use. Add the lemon juice and stir. Garnish with lemon peel.
(The ginger syrup will keep in the refrigerator for 6 months)

Arlene Guberman, Lyn, MA, USA

And Finally

The recipe for happiness
Is easy to prepare.
Take a pound of thoughtfulness
And mix it in with care.
Let it cool for just a while
Then add consideration.
Before it boils, take from the top
All anger and frustration.
Sprinkle with some sympathy
Flavour with happy smiles
And in it place a loving heart .
Wait till set then sprinkle seeds
Of kindle thoughts and willing deeds.
The ending should be complete success
Of human joy and happiness.

Jean Horncastle, Westward Ho!

Knitting Patterns

Gingerbread Men
(Pattern supplied by 'Simply Knitting')

D.K. Wool   No.4mm Needles
Knitted in one piece (Make2)

Left Leg

Cast on 7 sts
Row 1 P
Row 2 K2 tog. K4. Kfb.(Knit into front and back of st)
Rows 3,5,7 and 9 P
Rows 4,6,8 and 10 as row 2
Break yarn leaving leg on needle

Right Leg

Cast on 7 Sts
Row 1 P
Row 2 Kfb.K4.K2 tog
Rows 3,5,7 and 9 P
Rows4,6,8 and 10 as row 2

Slip sts of right leg onto a cable needle then slip onto needle holding left leg.
Both legs have wrong side facing on the left needle.
Re-join yarn, then purl across both legs

Body and Arms

Next Row K2 tog at both ends of row
Next Row P
Starting with a K row, work 7 rows st. st (1 Row K, 1RowP)
Next Row cast on 7sts P to end
Next Row cast on 7sts K to end
Starting with a P row work 6 rows st, st
Next Row cast off 7sts P to end
Next Row cast off 7sts K to end

Shoulders and Head

Next Row   P2 tog at both ends of row
Next Row   K2 tog at both ends of row
Next Row   P2 tog at both ends of row
Next Row   Kfb at both ends of row
Next Row   Pfb at both ends of row
Next Row   K at both ends of row
Next Row   Pfb at both ends of row
Next Row   K
Next Row   P
Next Row   K
Next Row   P2 tog at both ends of row
Next Row   K2 tog at both ends of row
Next Row   P
Next Row   K2 tog at both ends of row
Cast off purlwise.

Stitch up and stuff. Finish with embroidered eyes and mouth and sew on buttons

Cup Cakes

D.K 4mm Needles

<u>Cake Base</u>

Cast on 30 Sts
Knit 12 Rows
Next Row K2 tog across row 15 sts
Next Row K
Next Row K2 tog across row, K last st 8sts
Next Row K2 tog across row 4 sts
Next Row K2 tog across row 2 sts
Next Row K2 tog
Cast off
Sew side seams to form a cup shape

<u>Icing</u>

Cast on 12 sts
Work 12 rows in stocking st (1 row K) (1Row P)
Cast off

Put stuffing into cake base, then sew icing over the top of the cake base.
Decorate with beads, sequins (optional)

Alison Murray, Devon

Sweet

Cast on 16 Sts
Knit 8 rows in stocking st (1 row K) (1Row P)
Next Row K in front & back every st, 32 sts
K 8 Rows in s.s.
Next Row K2 tog across Row 16 sts
K 8 Rows in s.s.
Cast off, stuff and sew.

Alison Murray, N. Devon

Acknowledgments

We would like to thank everyone who has knitted, or contributed in any way to this project, because without all their hard work and generosity we could not have achieved such a fantastic result.
Special thanks to Mike Jubb who wrote the introductory poem especially for our recipe book and inspired the title.

Kindly sponsored by:

Atlantic Village Shopping Outlet, Bideford
The Big Sheep, Abbotsham
J H Taylor Fastenings, Roundswell
Webbers, Bideford
John Heathcoat Fabrics, Barnstaple
Jewson, Bideford

Knitters and helpers

Groups
2nd Bideford Brownies, Devon
Atherington & Umberleigh W.I.
Belper Guides, Derbyshire
Brook Valley W.I., E. Sussex
Chittlehampton Spiders, Devon
Coombe Martin Craft Club
Derbyshire NHS, Kingsway Hospital, Derby
Derbyshire Resource Centre Day Hospital, Derby
Dulverton & Brushford Craft Group
Dyffryn Clydach Knitathon, W Glamorgan

Eastern Green W.I., Coventry
Instow W.I., Devon
Krafty Tarts Craft Club, Bristol
Langton Craft Group
Mental Health Services for Older People, Plymouth
Newport (Shropshire) Townswomen's Guild
Nutty Knitters of Yeo Vale Road, Devon
Oreston Methodist Church, Plymouth
Prescot & District U3A Craft Group, Merseyside
Rawthorpe Junior School, Huddersfield
Retirement Fellowship, Northam, Devon
Spofforth W.I., N.Yorks
St Helens Primary School Knitting Club, Devon
Stroke Club & Helpers of Minehead
Supported Housing For The Elderly, Solihull
The Big Sheep Knitting Club
The Goat Girls of Builth Wells, Powys
The Knitting Bags of Rhode Island U.S.A.
West Buckland W.I.
West Somerset Stroke Club, Somerset
West Yorkshire Playhouse - Heydays Knitters
Weybridge United Reformed Church
Woking Evening Townswomens Guild

With apologies to anyone who we may have accidentally omitted or for any mis-spelt names or places.

Individuals

Ruth, Devon
Dot, Yeo Vale
Lillian, Yeo Vale
Little Joan, Yeo Vale
Mary, Yeo Vale
Rosemary, Yeo Vale

A

Gillian Adams, North Devon
Dr Alia Allim, Cardiff
Pam Almond, Somerset
Peg Anderson
Marilyn Anscombe, Devon
Claire Arnold
Emily Arnold
Jane Ashby, Kent
Mrs I.R. Ashdown, Devon
Mrs Jean Ashdown, Devon
Mrs B Ayre, E. Yorks

B

Mrs F.M. Bailey, E.Yorks
Mrs Lilian Bailey, Devon
Marie Bamberger, Bideford
Mrs Phyllis Bamforth, Lancs
Mrs Vera Banner, Devon
Mrs Dorothy Barber, Warwickshire
Mrs Elizabeth Barber, Warwickshire
Pauline Barber, West Yorkshire

Mrs Jean Barbour, Somerset
Mrs Alison Barker, Essex
Susan Barker, Lincs
Norma Barritt, Devon
Janet Barwood, Warwickshire
Sheena Battisson, Nottingham
Christine Bebbington, Gloucs
Mrs Lesley Beck, W. Yorks
Ruth Benney, Devon
Mrs Mary Bentley, Bedfordshire
Mrs Berryman, Cornwall
Marjorie Biggin, West Yorkshire
Phyl Billing, St Austell
Phyllis Billing, St Austell
Beryl Billings, Shropshire
Jackie Bishop, Northamptonshire
Mrs Margaret Blake, Surrey
Jennifer Blowfield, Leics
Mrs Liz Bolt, Cornwall
Janet Bonnick, Devon
Mrs Yvonne W Boone, Devon
Ann Boot, Vale of Glamorgan
Mrs S Bosworth, Birmingham
Jan Boughton, N.Devon
Anne Bound, W. Sussex
Susan Boutle, N. Devon
Mrs E.J. Bradshaw, South Devon
Joan & Jessica Brayley, Devon, Aged 11
Marilyn Breen, Devon
Brenda Briggs, N. Cornwall
Marion Brockett, Essex
Josie Bromley, Leicestershire
Mrs Irene Broom, Cornwall
Sue Browes, West Yorkshire

Diane Brunsdon, Hampshire
Mrs Linda Burke, Somerset
Vicki Burke, Merseyside
Linda Burton, Devon
Patricia Bushell & Cathy, W. Midlands

C

Joyce Carr, N.Devon
Mrs Judith Cartwright, West Yorkshire
Mrs Margaret Carver, West Yorkshire
Mrs Jude Casemore, N.Devon
Mrs Barbara Castle, Middlesex
Mrs S Castle, N. Devon
Mrs Christine Chapman, Lincolnshire
Edna Chapman, Hampshire
Mrs Stephanie Charnock, Beds
Anne Chenrolle
Johanna Chilcott, Devon
Helen Church, Mid Glamorgan
Vera Clark, W.Sussex
Jeanne Clarke, Devon
Karen Clarke, Devon
Phil Clarke, Devon
Karen & Ella Clarke, Devon
Mrs Clarkson, Devon
Winifred Clason, Devon
Mrs Evelyn Cockings, Suffolk
Mrs Linda Cockings, Essex
Mrs M.J. Cocks, W. Sussex
Mrs Joan Cohen
Margaret Cornish, North Devon
Joan Coils, Coventry
Mrs Margaret Cole, Peterborough
Tony A. Coles, S. Wales
Mrs Beryl Convery, N.Devon

Mrs Margaret Cook, Devon
Carol Cooke, Cornwall
Mrs S Coombe, Devon
Jacky Cooper, N.Yorks
Joan Cope, Berkshire
Mrs J Corbett, N.Devon
Mrs Elizabeth Corry, N. Ireland
Diana Couch, Cornwall
Mrs Mary Course, Devon
Eileen Critchley, Shropshire
Clarissa Harding-Crook, Devon
Thelma Crook, Devon
Mary Crowther
Margaret Cuff, Devon
Beth Currant, Beds
Carolyn Curtis, Devon
Mrs Joyce Curtis, Lincolnshire

D

Val Darby, Devon
Mrs Jean Davie, S.Devon
Sally Davie, Devon
Mrs M. Davies, Cornwall
Mrs E.M. Davies, Cornwall
Mrs Joy Davies, Cornwall
Mrs Jean Davis, Devon
Mrs K.I. Davis, Somerset
M Dawson, West Yorkshire
Mrs Linda Deakin, Worcs
Elizabeth Dinsmore, Quebec, Canada
Julie Distin, Staffs
Mrs M. Palmer-Douglas, Cornwall
Mrs Kathleen M. Drinkwater, Manchester
Mrs P Duncan, Cornwall

Enid Dunscombe, S.Glamorgan
Mary Dyer, Devon
Carl Dyke, Berks
Mrs Cynthia Dymond, N. Devon
Mrs Shirley Dyson, N.Yorks

E
Miss W.E. Eccles, Devon
Alex Edwards, West Midlands
Mrs Jean Edwards, Devon
Christine Hudson-Elkington, U.S.A.
Jo Elliot, Shropshire
Pam Elliott, Devon
Dee Ellis, Devon
Hazel Evans, Surrey

F
Astrid Manuel-Farmer, Devon
Mrs P Farmer, Leicester
Mrs Patricia R Farrow, Birmingham
Mrs Judy Fetherston, Norfolk
Jake & Lauren Fincken, Hants
Ishbel Finlayson, Aberdeenshire
Anne Finn, Surrey
Mrs Pauline Fisher, Essex
Mrs Peggy Fisk, Lincolnshire
Christine Forder,Devon
Joan Foster, Mersyside
Colin Frajbis, N. Devon
Mrs P.A. Francis, Devon
Pamela Freeman, Yorkshire
Abigail Freemantle, Devon
Mrs Joan Freer, Leeds
Jess Fubini, Devon

G

Mrs Margaret Gale, Devon
Mrs Jo Gammon, Devon
Miss M Gibb, Somerset
Shirley Gibson, West Yorkshire
Ann Gilbert, Pembrokeshire
Cath Gilbert, Stafford
Mrs Angela Gilsbody, N. Devon
Mrs Brenda Girling, E.Yorkshire
Mrs Margaret Glass, Devon
Muriel Gollop, Somerset
Mrs Jean Gooderson, Devon
Mrs Greta Goss, Devon
Rita Gould, Devon
Mrs Grant,Somerset
Marilyn Green, Bristol
Mrs Marion Green, Bucks
Mary Green, Devon
Joyce Griffiths, Pembrokeshire
Paulette Griffiths, Wolverhampton
Arlene Guberman, Massacheusets, U.S.A.

H

Mrs Edna Haffield, Essex
Susan Hale & Friends, Devon
Mrs Freda Hainsworth, Surrey
Mrs S Hale, Devon
Carol Halliday, Birmingham
Joshua Hamilton, Cornwall
Laura Hamilton, Cornwall
Beryl Hancock, Devon
Sarah Harbent, Herts
Mrs M Harcus, Newmarket
Mrs E Harding, N.Devon, Aged 92

Mrs E.M.G. Harper, Gloucs
Sue Harper, West Midlands
Trudy Harris, Somerset
Mrs L Harris & co, W. Sussex
Mrs W Harrison, Sheffield
Mrs J Hartnoll, North Devon
Mrs M Harwood, Cornwall
Nora Hawkshead, West Yorkshire
Gill Hayhoe, Devon
Beverley Heard, Devo
Mrs Jean Heard
Mrs Nancy Heard, Devon
Mrs Margaret Heath, Somerset
Jennifer Hedden, Devon
Mrs Doreen Hemsworth, Essex
Eunice Hewitt, Newport
Brenda Heywood, Devon
Mrs Pat Hibb, Surrey
Christine Higgins, Devon
Margaret Hill, West Yorkshire
Angie Hindson, N. Devon
Pat Hindson, N. Devon
JM Hitchon, Devon
Rosemary Hobson, Somerset
Mary Hole, Devon, Aged 91
Dian Holm, Lancs
Caroline Hordell, U.S.A.
Mrs Jean Horncastle, Devon
Mrs June Horrell, Devon
Sylvia Hosken
Mrs M.C. Housam, North Devon
Mrs L Hudson, N Devon
Miss M.I. Hudson, N.Devon
Teresa Hughes, Birmingham

Linda Hunkin, Cornwall
Mrs Joyce Hursey, Devon

I

Carol Ibbestson
Lorraine Irwin, Devon
Mrs Annie Isherwood, Somerset

J

Elsie Jeffery, Devon
Hilary L. Jenkin, Cornwall
Doreen Jennings, Beds
Dawn Jepson, Derby
Kelly Jepson, Derby
Olive Jepson, Derby
Jacqui Jessiman
Mrs Anne Johnson, Cheshire
Miss Sarah May Johnson, London
Val Johnson, Devon
Rosemary Joisce, Berkshire
Ann Jones, West Midlands
Anna Jones, Devon
Mrs Barbara Jones, Powys, Mid Wales
Mrs Pamela Jones, Pembrokeshire
Mike Jubb, Hants
Sally Jubb, Hants

K

Mrs Kay Kemp, Essex
Joan Kentshley
Dee King, Cornwall
Ivy King, Devon
Pamela Kirkham, West Yorkshire
Mrs A Klima, Devon

Joyce Knight, Bournemouth
Ellen Krupowicz, Rhode Island, U.S.A.

L

LMrs Betty Lakin, Staffs
Mrs Jeanette Lawrence
Beryl Lee, Coventry
Sheila Leishman, Berkshire
Jane Lewis, Herts
Michelle Lewis, Devon
Joshua Liddall, Devon
Mrs Angela Liddle, Lancs
Mrs Pauline Linrols, Berks
Anne Lintern, Somerset
Sheila Littlejohns, N.Devon
Judith Lobendhan, Surrey
Brenda Lomax, Devon
Francis Loughlin, Dorset
Sylvia Lovell, Devon
Margaret Lovelock, N.Devon
Mrs Caroline Lucas, N. Devon
Sue Lucas, Bristol
Eileen Luscombe, N.Devon

M

Mrs Eileen MacCaig, N. Devon
Mary MacDonald, West Yorkshire
Mrs M.R. Madge, Devon
Mrs Jacqueline Major, East Yorkshire
Maureen Mann, Devon
Mrs J Manning, Cornwall
Debbie Marais, Shropshire
Jessamy Marais, Shropshire
Mrs Margaret Marochan, Devon

Mrs Annie Marriott, Devon, Aged 90+
Wendy Armstrong-Marriott, Devon
Sue Marshall, Devon
Mrs Caroll Martin, Essex
Maureeen Martin, Devon
Pat Mather, Mersyside
Jacky Mathers, West Yorkshire
Mrs B Mathnick, Somerset
H McMillan, Ross-shire
Jean S McNeill, Surrey
Mrs P Mears
Barbara Miles, Somerset
Drusilla Millington, West Midlands
Mary Monk, Devon
Charlotte Moosa, N Devon
Jan Morford, Devon
Shirley Morgan, Shropshire
Babs Muir, Devon
Mrs Pearl Mullen, Devon
Devon Murdoch, Devon

N

Mrs L Need, Smethwick
Mrs M Nelmes, West Midlands
Mavis Newby, West Yorkshire
Mrs Hilary Newing, Devon
M Nutter, West Yorkshire

O

Rosie O'Callaghan, Devon
Sophie O'Callaghan, Devon
Mrs Pearl O'Donnell
Mrs Anne Olde, Devon
Margaret Mary O'Neil, U.S.A.

Mrs G Osborn, Warkwickshire
Mrs Rosemary Osborne, Devon
Mrs Una Osborne, Staffordshire

P

Mavis Page
Sheila Pallister, Cardiff
Norma Palmer, U.S.A.
Brenda Parker, Glos
Ms Brenda Parkin, Somerset
Mrs Lesley Parkin, Hampshire
Barbara Parr
Maureen Patmore, N.Devon
Mrs June Peace, Dorset
Patsy Pearce, Cornwall
Sarah Pedlar, Devon
Morag Peers, Oxford
Mrs Emma Peglar, Cornwall
Sandy Peters, N Devon
Mrs Kathy Phillips, Flintshire
Mrs Pat Phillips, N.Devon
Mrs Ray Phillips, Devon
Ann Pickett, Devon
Bridget Pike, Devon
Mrs Maureen Pilgrim, Berkshire
Mrs Joan E. Pine, Kent
Mrs Jenny Potts, Warwickshire
Mrs Joy Powell, Cornwall
Mrs B Prance, Devon
Mrs M Prescott, Somerset
Sheila Procter, West Yorkshire
May Prouse, Devon
Mrs Kate Purdy, Kent

Q
Audrey Quinn, Devon

R
Mary Rawlings
Doris Redclift, Devon
Mrs Rosalind Reed, Somerset
Barbara Reeves, West Midlands
Mrs Janet Richards, Selkirkshire
Bernadette Richardson, Lancs
Mrs Jan Richardson, Selkirkshire
Margaret Richardson, N. Yorks
Mrs J Rickards, Devon
Mrs Rosina Ridgeway, Cornwall
Janet Roberts, Walsall
Jenny Roberts, Oxford
Thelma Roberts, Surrey
Angela Roddick, Bristol
Maggie Rodgers, North Devon
Christine Rogers, Dorset
Mrs Nicola Roltpon, Gloucs
Anne Rood, Devon
Mrs E Rose, Birmingham
Edna Rose, West Yorkshire
Mrs Shirley Rossiter, Devon
Mrs Ivy Roy, Hants
Mrs Dorothy Rumbles, Berkshire

S
Mrs Hilary Sales, N.Devon
Gwen Salmon, N.Devon
Jennifer Sargent, N.Devon
Mrs Yvonne Sargent, N.Devon
Rev. Gerald Satterly, N. Cornwall
Mrs Margaret Satterly

Barbara Schweller, New York, U.S.A.
Linnie Seward, Devon
Susie Seward, Spain
Margaret Shaddick, N. Devon
Mrs Sandra Shanks, Norfolk
Val Sharpe, Devon
Elaine Sheriden
Monica Shorey, Devon
Mrs Jean Skinner, Warwickshire
Mrs E P Slaughter, Herts
Audrey Sleath, Cornwall
Mrs Jacqueline Smith, Leicester
Mrs Joyce P Smith, S. Yorks
Mrs Olive Smith, Warwickshire
Simone Smith, Kent
Mrs T Smith, Sheffield
Mrs Thelma Smith, Plymouth
Mrs V J Smith, N. Devon
Mrs Patricia Soby, N. Devon
Mrs C.R. Solomon, Bristol
Anne F.V. Spalding, Birmingham
Hazel Spencer, Dorset
Mrs R Spicer, Berks
Iris Spink, West Yorkshire
Brenda Stacey, N. Devon
D.M. Stanbury, Somerset
Vivienne Stell, West Yorkshire
Glenna Stephens, Hampshire
Mrs Ann Stevens, Hull
Christine Stevens, Somerset
Penny Stevenson, West Yorkshire
Mrs Jean Stickland, Dorset
Mrs Renee Stonehouse, Surrey
Mrs Phyllis Surgeon, Devon

Mrs JM Swinger, Swindon
Mrs Joan Sylvester, N. Devon

T

Jill Tarr, Halesowen
Samm Tarry, Northampton
Anne Tattersall, N. Devon
Mrs A Taylor, Derbyshire
Barbara Taylor, West Yorkshire
Mrs Joan Taylor, Coventry
Maureen Taylor, Wolverhampton
Alice May Taylor, Devon
Megan Taylor, Devon
B.E. Terrell, Devon
Angela Thames, Hampshire
Alison Thomas, West Glamorgan
Eryl Thomas, Mid Glamorgan
M.E. Thomas, Devon
Sheila Thomas, Devon
Leslie Thompson, Wiltshire
Georgina Thompson, Wiltshire
Penny Thompson, N. Devon
Mrs Carol Ann Thorn, Alicante, Spain
Mrs Joyce Thorn, Cornwall
Criss Thorne, Devon
Anne Thornton, Exeter
Mrs Jean Tovey, Nuneaton
Elaine Townsend, Nottingham
Mrs S Tripp, Devon
Mrs Marigold Truscot, Cornwall
Mrs Josephine Truscott, Gloucs
Mrs Doris Trussell, Surrey
Helena Turner, Cornwall
Mrs N Turner, Devon

V

Patricia Valentine, West Yorkshire
Mrs Ivy Voysey, Somerset

W

Max Wainwright, Harrogate, Aged 6
Jenny Walker, Devon
Teresa Waller, Cambs
Judith Ward, Somerset
Mrs Julie Ward, Birmingham
Mrs J Warkling, Coventry
Matina Warner, Coventry
Mrs Rita Watcham, N. Yorks
Jennifer Wear, Cumbria
Julie Wear, Cumbria
Valerie Westlake, Devon
Claire Westrop, Mid Glamorgan
Barbara Whitehouse, Devon
Jenny Whitmarsh, Devon
Mary Wilcox, Devon
Mrs Maureen B Willetts, West Midlands
Mrs Diane Williams Kent
Mrs Gayle Wilson, Worcs
Hazel Wonnacott, Devon
Ivy Woods, Berks
Jan Wooley, West Midlands
Joyce Wooley, Birmingham
Mrs Lesley Wright, Dorset

Y

Fiona Yelland, Devon
Holly Yelland, Devon, Aged 10
Jean Yeoman, West Yorkshire

Notes

Notes

Notes